Sometimes a job seems so big
and you seem so little.
But a little goes a long way when . . .

Text by Lois Rock
Text copyright © 1996 Lion Publishing
Illustrations copyright © 1996 Roger Langton

The author asserts the moral right
to be identified as the author of this work

Published by
Lion Publishing plc
Sandy Lane West, Oxford, England
ISBN 0 7459 3105 7
Lion Publishing
4050 Lee Vance Road, Colorado Springs, CO 80918, USA
ISBN 0 7459 3105 7
Albatross Books Pty Ltd
PO Box 320, Sutherland, NSW 2232, Australia
ISBN 0 7324 0965 9

First edition 1996
10 9 8 7 6 5 4 3 2 1 0

A catalogue for this book
is available from the British Library

Library of Congress CIP data applied for
Printed and bound in Singapore

**This retelling is based on the stories
of Jesus' life in the Bible.**

Jesus Shares a Picnic

Retold by Lois Rock
Illustrations by Roger Langton

A LION BOOK

Crowds followed Jesus wherever he went. One day, he wanted to be alone for a while.

Jesus and his close friends got into a boat and sailed across Lake Galilee.

But the crowds came hurrying down to the shore on the other side of the lake.

Some were sick: they wanted to be healed. Some had questions about God: they wanted to hear what Jesus had to say.

Jesus welcomed them.

He let the people stay all day—until
the sun was beginning to set.

But by now they were hungry. What would it cost to feed all those people? Lots and lots and lots.

Jesus' close friends were worried. They didn't have that kind of money.

Did they have anything to offer? "Well yes," said one of Jesus' friends—a man named Andrew.

"A boy here has five loaves of flat barley bread and two fish."

A picnic for one.

And five thousand hungry people.

"Tell the people to sit down," said Jesus.

So everyone sat down on the grass.

Jesus took the bread. "Thank you God, for this bread," he said.

And he handed it out to the people close by.

Then he took the fish. "Thank you, God, for these fish," he said.

And he handed those out too.

People took the food from the person next to them.

They broke off a bit for themselves,
and passed the rest on.

And on. And on. And on.

Everyone had as much as they wanted.

When the eating was over, Jesus asked his friends to gather up the scraps.

The leftovers filled twelve baskets.

A Christian prayer

Dear God,
You notice little children.
You notice what they have
and what they can do.
Please use the things I have
and the things I can do—
and do wonderful things with them!
Amen.